Personal Information	
Name:	Date of Birth:
Adress:	
Business Adress:	
Email:	
Mobile Telephone:	
Home Telephone:	
Fax:	

Emergency Contact	
Name:	Relationship:
Adress:	
Mobile Telephone:	
Home Telephone:	
Email:	

Notes

<table>
<tr><td colspan="2" align="center">Vehicle Information</td></tr>
<tr><td>Vehicle:</td><td>Year:</td></tr>
<tr><td colspan="2">Make:</td></tr>
<tr><td colspan="2">Model:</td></tr>
<tr><td colspan="2">Engine:</td></tr>
<tr><td colspan="2">VIN Number:</td></tr>
<tr><td>Purchase Date:</td><td>Mileage at Purchase:</td></tr>
<tr><td colspan="2">Purchase Form:</td></tr>
</table>

<table>
<tr><td colspan="2" align="center">Insurance Company</td></tr>
<tr><td colspan="2">Company Name:</td></tr>
<tr><td colspan="2">Adress:</td></tr>
<tr><td colspan="2"></td></tr>
<tr><td>Office:</td><td>Work:</td></tr>
<tr><td>Phone:</td><td>Fax:</td></tr>
<tr><td colspan="2">Email:</td></tr>
<tr><td colspan="2">Website:</td></tr>
<tr><td>Agent:</td><td>Phone:</td></tr>
<tr><td colspan="2">Cost:</td></tr>
<tr><td colspan="2">Insurance Numbre:</td></tr>
<tr><td colspan="2">Cover Details:</td></tr>
<tr><td>Start Date:</td><td>End Date:</td></tr>
</table>

<table>
<tr><td align="center">Notes</td></tr>
<tr><td></td></tr>
<tr><td></td></tr>
<tr><td></td></tr>
<tr><td></td></tr>
<tr><td></td></tr>
<tr><td></td></tr>
</table>

YEAR: __________   MONTH: __________   MODEL: __________

Date / Time	Oil Changed	Air Filter	Balance Tires	Wheel Alignment	Fuel Filter	Brakes Serviced	Spark Plugs	Transmission	Wiper Blades	Batteries	Radiator	Belts&Hoses	Mileage

make: date purchased:

model: purchased price:

license plate: purchased form:

Date/Time	Maintenance/Comments	Mileage

YEAR: ____________ MONTH: ____________ MODEL: ____________

Date / Time	Oil Changed	Air Filter	Balance Tires	Wheel Alignment	Fuel Filter	Brakes Serviced	Spark Plugs	Transmission	Wiper Blades	Batteries	Radiator	Belts&Horses	Mileage

make: _________________________ date purchased: _________________________

model: _________________________ purchased price: _________________________

license plate: _________________________ purchased form: _________________________

Date/Time	Maintenance/Comments	Mileage

YEAR: _________   MONTH: _________   MODEL: _________

Date / Time	Oil Changed	Air Filter	Balance Tires	Wheel Alignment	Fuel Filter	Brakes Serviced	Spark Plugs	Transmission	Wiper Blades	Batteries	Radiator	Belts&Hoses	Mileage

make:		date purchased:
model:		purchased price:
license plate:		purchased form:

Date/Time	Maintenance/Comments	Mileage

YEAR: __________   MONTH: __________   MODEL: __________

Date / Time	Oil Changed	Air Filter	Balance Tires	Wheel Alignment	Fuel Filter	Brakes Serviced	Spark Plugs	Transmission	Wiper Blades	Batteries	Radiator	Belts&Horses	Mileage

make: ___________________________   date purchased: ___________________________

model: ___________________________   purchased price: ___________________________

license plate: ___________________________   purchased form: ___________________________

Date/Time	Maintenance/Comments	Mileage

make: ___________________________

model: ___________________________

YEAR: _________ MONTH: _________ MODEL: _________

Date / Time	Oil Changed	Air Filter	Balance Tires	Wheel Alignment	Fuel Filter	Brakes Serviced	Spark Plugs	Transmission	Wiper Blades	Batteries	Radiator	Belts&Horses	Mileage

Date/Time	Maintenance/Comments	Mileage

YEAR: _________ MONTH: _________ MODEL: _________

Date / Time	Oil Changed	Air Filter	Balance Tires	Wheel Alignment	Fuel Filter	Brakes Serviced	Spark Plugs	Transmission	Wiper Blades	Batteries	Radiator	Belts&Hoses	Mileage

make: ____________________   date purchased: ____________________

model: ____________________   purchased price: ____________________

license plate: ____________________   purchased form: ____________________

Date/Time	Maintenance/Comments	Mileage

Date / Time	Oil Changed	Air Filter	Balance Tires	Wheel Alignment	Fuel Filter	Brakes Serviced	Spark Plugs	Transmission	Wiper Blades	Batteries	Radiator	Belts&Hoses	Mileage

make: _______________________   date purchased: _______________________

model: _______________________   purchased price: _______________________

license plate: _______________________   purchased form: _______________________

Date/Time	Maintenance/Comments	Mileage

YEAR: _______   MONTH: _______   MODEL: _______

Date / Time	Oil Changed	Air Filter	Balance Tires	Wheel Alignment	Fuel Filter	Brakes Serviced	Spark Plugs	Transmission	Wiper Blades	Batteries	Radiator	Belts&Hoses	Mileage

Date / Time	Oil Changed	Air Filter	Balance Tires	Wheel Alignment	Fuel Filter	Brakes Serviced	Spark Plugs	Transmission	Wiper Blades	Batteries	Radiator	Belts&Hoses	Mileage

make: _______________________   date purchased: _______________________

model: _______________________   purchased price: _______________________

license plate: _______________________   purchased form: _______________________

Date/Time	Maintenance/Comments	Mileage

YEAR: _________   MONTH: _________   MODEL: _________

Date / Time	Oil Changed	Air Filter	Balance Tires	Wheel Alignment	Fuel Filter	Brakes Serviced	Spark Plugs	Transmission	Wiper Blades	Batteries	Radiator	Belts&Hoses	Mileage

make: date purchased:

model: purchased price:

license plate: purchased form:

Date/Time	Maintenance/Comments	Mileage

make:

model:

YEAR: _________ MONTH: _________ MODEL: _________

Mileage

Date/Time	Oil Changed	Air Filter	Balance Tires	Wheel Alignment	Fuel Filter	Brakes Serviced	Spark Plugs	Transmission	Wiper Blades	Batteries	Radiator	Belts&Hoses	Mileage

make: _______________________   date purchased: _______________________

model: _______________________   purchased price: _______________________

license plate: _______________________   purchased form: _______________________

Date/Time	Maintenance/Comments	Mileage

YEAR: __________   MONTH: __________   MODEL: __________

Date / Time	Oil Changed	Air Filter	Balance Tires	Wheel Alignment	Fuel Filter	Brakes Serviced	Spark Plugs	Transmission	Wiper Blades	Batteries	Radiator	Belts&Hoses	Mileage

make: _______________________   date purchased: _______________________

model: _______________________   purchased price: _______________________

license plate: _______________________   purchased form: _______________________

Date/Time	Maintenance/Comments	Mileage

YEAR: _________ MONTH: _________ MODEL: _________

Date/Time	Oil Changed	Air Filter	Balance Tires	Wheel Alignment	Fuel Filter	Brakes Serviced	Spark Plugs	Transmission	Wiper Blades	Batteries	Radiator	Belts&Hoses	Mileage

make: _______________________   date purchased: _______________________

model: _______________________   purchased price: _______________________

license plate: _______________________   purchased form: _______________________

Date/Time	Maintenance/Comments	Mileage

YEAR: __________   MONTH: __________   MODEL: __________

Date / Time	Oil Changed	Air Filter	Balance Tires	Wheel Alignment	Fuel Filter	Brakes Serviced	Spark Plugs	Transmission	Wiper Blades	Batteries	Radiator	Belts&Hoses	Mileage

make: ______________________ date purchased: ______________________

model: ______________________ purchased price: ______________________

license plate: ______________________ purchased form: ______________________

Date/Time	Maintenance/Comments	Mileage

YEAR: _________ MONTH: _________ MODEL: _________

Date / Time	Oil Changed	Air Filter	Balance Tires	Wheel Alignment	Fuel Filter	Brakes Serviced	Spark Plugs	Transmission	Wiper Blades	Batteries	Radiator	Belts&Hoses	Mileage

make: _______________________   date purchased: _______________________

model: _______________________   purchased price: _______________________

license plate: _______________________   purchased form: _______________________

Date/Time	Maintenance/Comments	Mileage

YEAR: __________ MONTH: __________ MODEL: __________

Date/Time	Oil Changed	Air Filter	Balance Tires	Wheel Alignment	Fuel Filter	Brakes Serviced	Spark Plugs	Transmission	Wiper Blades	Batteries	Radiator	Belts&Hoses	Mileage

| Date/Time | Oil Changed | Air Filter | Balance Tires | Wheel Alignment | Fuel Filter | Brakes Serviced | Spark Plugs | Transmission | Wiper Blades | Batteries | Radiator | Belts&Hoses |

make: ___________________   date purchased: ___________________

model: ___________________   purchased price: ___________________

license plate: ___________________   purchased form: ___________________

Date/Time	Maintenance/Comments	Mileage

YEAR: ___________ MONTH: ___________ MODEL: ___________

Date / Time	Oil Changed	Air Filter	Balance Tires	Wheel Alignment	Fuel Filter	Brakes Serviced	Spark Plugs	Transmission	Wiper Blades	Batteries	Radiator	Belts&Hoses	Mileage

make:	date purchased:
model:	purchased price:
license plate:	purchased form:

Date/Time	Maintenance/Comments	Mileage

YEAR: _______ MONTH: _______ MODEL: _______

Date / Time	Oil Changed	Air Filter	Balance Tires	Wheel Alignment	Fuel Filter	Brakes Serviced	Spark Plugs	Transmission	Wiper Blades	Batteries	Radiator	Belts&Hoses	Mileage

make: date purchased:

model: purchased price:

license plate: purchased form:

Date/Time	Maintenance/Comments	Mileage

YEAR: __________ MONTH: __________ MODEL: __________

Date / Time	Oil Changed	Air Filter	Balance Tires	Wheel Alignment	Fuel Filter	Brakes Serviced	Spark Plugs	Transmission	Wiper Blades	Batteries	Radiator	Belts&Horses	Mileage

make: _______________________   date purchased: _______________________

model: _______________________   purchased price: _______________________

license plate: _______________________   purchased form: _______________________

Date/Time	Maintenance/Comments	Mileage

YEAR: _________ MONTH: _________ MODEL: _________

Date / Time	Oil Changed	Air Filter	Balance Tires	Wheel Alignment	Fuel Filter	Brakes Serviced	Spark Plugs	Transmission	Wiper Blades	Batteries	Radiator	Belts&Hoses	Mileage

make:	date purchased:
model:	purchased price:
license plate:	purchased form:

Date/Time	Maintenance/Comments	Mileage

YEAR: _____________ MONTH: _____________ MODEL: _____________

Date / Time	Oil Changed	Air Filter	Balance Tires	Wheel Alignment	Fuel Filter	Brakes Serviced	Spark Plugs	Transmission	Wiper Blades	Batteries	Radiator	Belts&Hoses	Mileage

make:	date purchased:
model:	purchased price:
license plate:	purchased form:

Date/Time	Maintenance/Comments	Mileage

YEAR: ____________ MONTH: ____________ MODEL: ____________

Date / Time	Oil Changed	Air Filter	Balance Tires	Wheel Alignment	Fuel Filter	Brakes Serviced	Spark Plugs	Transmission	Wiper Blades	Batteries	Radiator	Belts&Hoses	Mileage

make: ______________________________ date purchased: ______________________

model: _____________________________ purchased price: ______________________

license plate: _______________________ purchased form: ______________________

Date/Time	Maintenance/Comments	Mileage

make: ______________________________

model: _____________________________

YEAR: _______________ MONTH: _______________ MODEL: _______________

Date / Time	Oil Changed	Air Filter	Balance Tires	Wheel Alignment	Fuel Filter	Brakes Serviced	Spark Plugs	Transmission	Wiper Blades	Batteries	Radiator	Belts&Hoses	Mileage

make: date purchased:

model: purchased price:

license plate: purchased form:

Date/Time	Maintenance/Comments	Mileage

YEAR: _______   MONTH: _______   MODEL: _______

Date / Time	Oil Changed	Air Filter	Balance Tires	Wheel Alignment	Fuel Filter	Brakes Serviced	Spark Plugs	Transmission	Wiper Blades	Batteries	Radiator	Belts&Hoses	Mileage

make: _______________________   date purchased: _______________________

model: _______________________   purchased price: _______________________

license plate: _______________________   purchased form: _______________________

Date/Time	Maintenance/Comments	Mileage

YEAR: ______________ MONTH: ______________ MODEL: ______________

Date / Time	Oil Changed	Air Filter	Balance Tires	Wheel Alignment	Fuel Filter	Brakes Serviced	Spark Plugs	Transmission	Wiper Blades	Batteries	Radiator	Belts&Hoses	Mileage

make: ___________________   date purchased: ___________________

model: ___________________   purchased price: ___________________

license plate: ___________________ purchased form: ___________________

Date/Time	Maintenance/Comments	Mileage

YEAR: _______ MONTH: _______ MODEL: _______

Date / Time	Oil Changed	Air Filter	Balance Tires	Wheel Alignment	Fuel Filter	Brakes Serviced	Spark Plugs	Transmission	Wiper Blades	Batteries	Radiator	Belts&Hoses	Mileage

| Date / Time | Oil Changed | Air Filter | Balance Tires | Wheel Alignment | Fuel Filter | Brakes Serviced | Spark Plugs | Transmission | Wiper Blades | Batteries | Radiator | Belts&Hoses |

make: _______________________   date purchased: _______________________

model: _______________________   purchased price: _______________________

license plate: _______________________   purchased form: _______________________

Date/Time	Maintenance/Comments	Mileage

YEAR: __________   MONTH: __________   MODEL: __________

Date / Time	Oil Changed	Air Filter	Balance Tires	Wheel Alignment	Fuel Filter	Brakes Serviced	Spark Plugs	Transmission	Wiper Blades	Batteries	Radiator	Belts&Horses	Mileage

make: _______________________   date purchased: _______________________

model: _______________________   purchased price: _______________________

license plate: _______________________   purchased form: _______________________

Date/Time	Maintenance/Comments	Mileage

make: _______________________

model: _______________________

YEAR: __________ MONTH: __________ MODEL: __________

Date / Time	Oil Changed	Air Filter	Balance Tires	Wheel Alignment	Fuel Filter	Brakes Serviced	Spark Plugs	Transmission	Wiper Blades	Batteries	Radiator	Belts&Horses	Mileage

make: ________________________   date purchased: ________________

model: _______________________   purchased price: ________________

license plate: ________________   purchased form: ________________

Date/Time	Maintenance/Comments	Mileage

YEAR: _________ MONTH: _________ MODEL: _________

Date / Time	Oil Changed	Air Filter	Balance Tires	Wheel Alignment	Fuel Filter	Brakes Serviced	Spark Plugs	Transmission	Wiper Blades	Batteries	Radiator	Belts&Hoses	Mileage

make: _________________________   date purchased: _________________________

model: _________________________   purchased price: _________________________

license plate: _________________________   purchased form: _________________________

Date/Time	Maintenance/Comments	Mileage

YEAR: _________ MONTH: _________ MODEL: _________

Date / Time	Oil Changed	Air Filter	Balance Tires	Wheel Alignment	Fuel Filter	Brakes Serviced	Spark Plugs	Transmission	Wiper Blades	Batteries	Radiator	Belts&Hoses	Mileage

make: ___________________________   date purchased: ___________________________

model: ___________________________   purchased price: ___________________________

license plate: ___________________________   purchased form: ___________________________

Date/Time	Maintenance/Comments	Mileage

YEAR: _______________ MONTH: _______________ MODEL: _______________

Date / Time	Oil Changed	Air Filter	Balance Tires	Wheel Alignment	Fuel Filter	Brakes Serviced	Spark Plugs	Transmission	Wiper Blades	Batteries	Radiator	Belts&Hoses	Mileage

make: _______________________   date purchased: _______________

model: ______________________   purchased price: _______________

license plate: ______________   purchased form: _______________

Date/Time	Maintenance/Comments	Mileage

YEAR: _________   MONTH: _________   MODEL: _________

Date/Time	Oil Changed	Air Filter	Balance Tires	Wheel Alignment	Fuel Filter	Brakes Serviced	Spark Plugs	Transmission	Wiper Blades	Batteries	Radiator	Belts&Hoses	Mileage

make: _______________________   date purchased: _______________________

model: _______________________   purchased price: _______________________

license plate: _______________________   purchased form: _______________________

Date/Time	Maintenance/Comments	Mileage

YEAR: _______ MONTH: _______ MODEL: _______

Date / Time	Oil Changed	Air Filter	Balance Tires	Wheel Alignment	Fuel Filter	Brakes Serviced	Spark Plugs	Transmission	Wiper Blades	Batteries	Radiator	Belts&Hoses	Mileage

make: _______________________   date purchased: _______________________

model: _______________________   purchased price: _______________________

license plate: _______________________   purchased form: _______________________

Date/Time	Maintenance/Comments	Mileage

YEAR: _________ MONTH: _________ MODEL: _________

Date / Time	Oil Changed	Air Filter	Balance Tires	Wheel Alignment	Fuel Filter	Brakes Serviced	Spark Plugs	Transmission	Wiper Blades	Batteries	Radiator	Belts&Hoses	Mileage

make: _______________________   date purchased: _______________________

model: _______________________   purchased price: _______________________

license plate: _______________________   purchased form: _______________________

Date/Time	Maintenance/Comments	Mileage

YEAR: ______________ MONTH: ______________ MODEL: ______________

Date / Time	Oil Changed	Air Filter	Balance Tires	Wheel Alignment	Fuel Filter	Brakes Serviced	Spark Plugs	Transmission	Wiper Blades	Batteries	Radiator	Belts&Hoses	Mileage

make: _________________________   date purchased: _________________________

model: _________________________   purchased price: _________________________

license plate: _________________________   purchased form: _________________________

Date/Time	Maintenance/Comments	Mileage

YEAR: __________ MONTH: __________ MODEL: __________

Date / Time	Oil Changed	Air Filter	Balance Tires	Wheel Alignment	Fuel Filter	Brakes Serviced	Spark Plugs	Transmission	Wiper Blades	Batteries	Radiator	Belts&Hoses	Mileage

make: date purchased:

model: purchased price:

license plate: purchased form:

Date/Time	Maintenance/Comments	Mileage

YEAR: ________ MONTH: ________ MODEL: ________

Date / Time	Oil Changed	Air Filter	Balance Tires	Wheel Alignment	Fuel Filter	Brakes Serviced	Spark Plugs	Transmission	Wiper Blades	Batteries	Radiator	Belts&Hoses	Mileage

make: _____________________   date purchased: _____________________

model: _____________________   purchased price: _____________________

license plate: _____________________   purchased form: _____________________

Date/Time	Maintenance/Comments	Mileage

YEAR: _________   MONTH: _________   MODEL: _________

Date / Time	Oil Changed	Air Filter	Balance Tires	Wheel Alignment	Fuel Filter	Brakes Serviced	Spark Plugs	Transmission	Wiper Blades	Batteries	Radiator	Belts&Hoses	Mileage

make: _______________________   date purchased: _______________________

model: _______________________   purchased price: _______________________

license plate: _______________________   purchased form: _______________________

Date/Time	Maintenance/Comments	Mileage

make: _______________________

model: _______________________

YEAR: _________   MONTH: _________   MODEL: _________

Date / Time	Oil Changed	Air Filter	Balance Tires	Wheel Alignment	Fuel Filter	Brakes Serviced	Spark Plugs	Transmission	Wiper Blades	Batteries	Radiator	Belts&Horses	Mileage

make: ___________________________   date purchased: ___________________

model: __________________________   purchased price: __________________

license plate: ____________________   purchased form: __________________

Date/Time	Maintenance/Comments	Mileage

YEAR: ________   MONTH: ________   MODEL: ________

Date/Time	Oil Changed	Air Filter	Balance Tires	Wheel Alignment	Fuel Filter	Brakes Serviced	Spark Plugs	Transmission	Wiper Blades	Batteries	Radiator	Belts&Hoses	Mileage

| Date/Time | Oil Changed | Air Filter | Balance Tires | Wheel Alignment | Fuel Filter | Brakes Serviced | Spark Plugs | Transmission | Wiper Blades | Batteries | Radiator | Belts&Hoses | |

make: _______________________   date purchased: _______________________

model: _______________________   purchased price: _______________________

license plate: _______________________   purchased form: _______________________

Date/Time	Maintenance/Comments	Mileage

YEAR: __________   MONTH: __________   MODEL: __________

Date / Time	Oil Changed	Air Filter	Balance Tires	Wheel Alignment	Fuel Filter	Brakes Serviced	Spark Plugs	Transmission	Wiper Blades	Batteries	Radiator	Belts&Hoses	Mileage

make: date purchased:

model: purchased price:

license plate: purchased form:

Date/Time	Maintenance/Comments	Mileage

YEAR: __________ MONTH: __________ MODEL: __________

Date / Time	Oil Changed	Air Filter	Balance Tires	Wheel Alignment	Fuel Filter	Brakes Serviced	Spark Plugs	Transmission	Wiper Blades	Batteries	Radiator	Belts&Hoses	Mileage

make: _____________________________   date purchased: _____________________________

model: _____________________________   purchased price: _____________________________

license plate: _____________________________   purchased form: _____________________________

Date/Time	Maintenance/Comments	Mileage

YEAR: _________   MONTH: _________   MODEL: _________

Date / Time	Oil Changed	Air Filter	Balance Tires	Wheel Alignment	Fuel Filter	Brakes Serviced	Spark Plugs	Transmission	Wiper Blades	Batteries	Radiator	Belts&Horses	Mileage

make:		date purchased:
model:		purchased price:
license plate:		purchased form:

Date/Time	Maintenance/Comments	Mileage

YEAR: _________   MONTH: _________   MODEL: _________

Date / Time	Oil Changed	Air Filter	Balance Tires	Wheel Alignment	Fuel Filter	Brakes Serviced	Spark Plugs	Transmission	Wiper Blades	Batteries	Radiator	Belts&Hoses	Mileage

make: _______________   date purchased: _______________

model: ______________   purchased price: _______________

license plate: ________   purchased form: _______________

DATE/TIME	MAINTENANCE/COMMENTS	MILEAGE

YEAR: ________ MONTH: ________ MODEL: ________

Date / Time	Oil Changed	Air Filter	Balance Tires	Wheel Alignment	Fuel Filter	Brakes Serviced	Spark Plugs	Transmission	Wiper Blades	Batteries	Radiator	Belts&Hoses	Mileage

make: _______________________   date purchased: _______________________

model: _______________________   purchased price: _______________________

license plate: _______________________   purchased form: _______________________

Date/Time	Maintenance/Comments	Mileage

YEAR: ___________ MONTH: ___________ MODEL: ___________

Date / Time	Oil Changed	Air Filter	Balance Tires	Wheel Alignment	Fuel Filter	Brakes Serviced	Spark Plugs	Transmission	Wiper Blades	Batteries	Radiator	Belts&Hoses	Mileage

make: _______________________   date purchased: _______________________

model: _______________________   purchased price: _______________________

license plate: _______________________   purchased form: _______________________

Date/Time	Maintenance/Comments	Mileage

YEAR: _______ MONTH: _______ MODEL: _______

Date / Time	Oil Changed	Air Filter	Balance Tires	Wheel Alignment	Fuel Filter	Brakes Serviced	Spark Plugs	Transmission	Wiper Blades	Batteries	Radiator	Belts&Hoses	Mileage

make: ___________________   date purchased: ___________________

model: ___________________   purchased price: ___________________

license plate: ___________________   purchased form: ___________________

Date/Time	Maintenance/Comments	Mileage

YEAR: ___________ MONTH: ___________ MODEL: ___________

Date / Time	Oil Changed	Air Filter	Balance Tires	Wheel Alignment	Fuel Filter	Brakes Serviced	Spark Plugs	Transmission	Wiper Blades	Batteries	Radiator	Belts&Hoses	Mileage

YEARLY SUMMARY

month	total distance	total cost of fuel	total repairs	total maint.
jan				
feb				
mar				
apr				
may				
jun				
jul				
aug				
sep				
oct				
nov				
dec				

Thank you!

WE ARE GLAD THAT YOU PURCHASED OUR
BOOK!
PLEASE LET US KNOW HOW WE CAN IMPROVE IT!
YOUR FEEDBACK IS ESSENTIAL TO US.

Contact us at:

 log'Sin@gmail.com

---

JUST TITLE THE EMAIL 'CREATIVE' AND WE WILL

GIVE YOU SOME EXTRA SURPRISES!

www.ingramcontent.com/pod-product-compliance
Lightning Source LLC
LaVergne TN
LVHW020918200726
843506LV00011B/1745